Millionaire habits

Step-by-step guide to learning what wealthy people do to get richer

Roger Lee

Copyright © 2020

Roger Lee

DEDICATION

To my wife Eleanor
who supports all my foolish ideas,
to her eyes and her smile.

With the wish to never stop following your dreams.

Table of contents

THE HABITS **7**

MASTERY HABITS **19**

THE VALUE HABITS **28**

BUSINESS HABITS **43**

PERSONAL PRODUCTIVITY HABIT **65**

PEOPLE'S SKILL **83**

THE HABIT OF CHARACTER AND LEADERSHIP **97**

Introduction

Hello,

Because you have this powerful mind-blowing tool right now in your hands in form of a go, it leaves an impression that you are truly pressing and willing to discover what it takes to make the most out of your life, and I celebrate that about you. After several years of questioning, study and research, I decided to pen down my discoveries about the high flyers of this world, those who have made a name and build legacies, what they did with their time, what marked their turning moments, and the qualities that gave them the results they have.

Today, whenever young people speak of the future, you find them speak of it as though being successful is definitely something they will experience. In addition, when you ask the old people living in poverty and lack today, you would discover that there was a time they, just as all young blood speak about success, spoke of it too. In other words, being optimistic about success is not enough to make you successful; there are things you must do, habits you must establish, sacrifices you must make. When you absent yourself from these things, no matter how much you want, success you will not get it.

This book is a compendium of several research questions and

answers from some of the world's top entrepreneurs, athletics, artists, musicians, politicians, and the likes; what made them who they are today, how they got there, and how you too can make your way to that position of wealth.

Are you ready?

Let us go.

Where it all begins

Whatever is admirable to your eyes today is a product of individual and several efforts, it would be a lie to think being a millionaire is an easy feat anyone can just pull, especially when you had to grow to take a leap from below. There is a starting point to it, a trail to follow, a path to tow. Whoever you find today with some million dollars in the bank has a journey, they did not wake up successful, they grew into it, and this makes the experience a journey worth trying for everyone. You need to understudy what people of substance do to gain substance.

Questioning assumptions

We all came into this world as clean slates, devoid of knowledge, wisdom, skill, or attitude, and because we did not know anything, nature demanded that we depend on someone –our parents, siblings, or extended family –to take care of us. As we grew older, we began to watch and ask questions, and, whatever we were told, we took as truth. We held onto these ideas and would even argue with our friends about how wrong what they knew was and why they needed to chill out because their idea does not make sense, I mean how could "mummy be wrong? She knows everything there is".

Mind shaping conversations

Over time, as we begin to live with these ideas, philosophy and assumptions, we began to live them out because that is what we believe. This is why you will find that the children of the rich often roll with fellow rich kids in the neighborhood, the poor doing the same. When you get to speak with the children of the rich, a lot of things they say totally differs from what you hear from poor kids, such as their approach towards savings, money, friendship, government. Although they both are talking about the same topic, they hold a different perspective. This is as a result of their upbringing, the people they have listened to, the degree to which they have grown to believe those things and the role they currently play in their lives.

The difference between financial bondage and financial freedom is sometimes as simple as a set of assumptions people have held to be true because someone they respected or an experience they had in the past threw it at them and they believed it. This is why we all have the responsibility to question our personal and collective assumptions and philosophy about the things we have all come to believe. For instance, if you have been trying to get rich and everything you believe (and have gone ahead to try) did not work out, isn't it enough for you to pause yourself and question those things? Do not be so engrossed with the things you have been taught or have come to believe, that you fail to realise that their time is up and should thus be abandoned. This was the light that guided the path to this book.

The pages of these books present ideas that will challenge what you have known and believed. I advise that you be critical in your thinking, I urge that you learn with an open mind and, wherever you find an idea that is superior to something you previously believed in, adopt it and run with it.

The end point of information

Learning about something does not automatically translate to results. It takes process, zeal, sweat and pain. If you go in the streets today, you will find broke walking dictionaries, you will know everything that is to be known about something but you will not find the results around them. People articulate other people's shortcomings, like its news report, the system, government, but they cannot point out something they did to either change their own lives or that of others. This is because although they acquired the tool, they never bothered to use it. The goal of knowledge is meant to be execution, which is the true test of knowledge. You cannot authenticate an idea that has not been tested; if you say that something works, you have to be able to prove it.

In science, there is no conclusion without experiment, everything from hypothesis, since data and assumptions are there to aid the experiment, no matter how much data a scientist accumulates or the hypothesis he or she creates, as long as they have not been put to test, an experiment has not been conducted. Knowing is not enough, you must do.

Why go through all this?

Well, this may have erupted some internal inquiry from you, asking "why sharing all this? Why don't we just go straight to the point; let's get to know these habits and be done with it!"

Well my friend, even if all I have been sharing here may not appear to be important to you, but it is actually the most important part of this book, which is where it all begins: the mind. It is important to get to the root of whatever challenge it may be, since being rich is more of an unconscious process than what we do consciously itself.

When habits are in their initial stage, you learn to do them consciously. For example, when a baby is about to walk, you will find that baby consciously trying to lift one leg over the other. Sometimes he trips, falls and starts all over again, sometimes he holds on some iron bar, couch, bucket, leans on the wall as he walks and tries to stand on his own. As time goes on, he no longer needs anything to help him stand, but there are limits to how long he can do that. His bones get stronger, he walks longer now, and then one day, you realize the baby is walking well, like every other human being. This time, he does it just well as if he had been walking for years; he does it as if there had never been a time he struggled to walk, to get up, lean on the wall so that he does not fall off.

Moving from being someone who is struggling financially to one who has experienced freedom is just like a child trying to walk; you have to do it consciously and then move into the unconscious space, which also accounts for why the poor struggle to be rich. The poor usually does not want to go through the process of consciously understanding how money works, the economics of wealth, as they refuse to lean on the walls of insights and carry baby steps as simple as saving at least 10% of their income.

I am sure you are getting some value already, but this is nothing compared to the many other values I have embedded in the pages of this book.

Chapter one

The habits

Habits have a strong role in the making of people, wherever you find people who are broke, check their habit, which is poor. Additionally, when you find someone who is successful too, check their daily routine, and you will discover the secrets too. One of the easiest ways to figure out a man's problem is to check his daily routine; what he does when he wakes up, how he spends his money, where he hangs out, and who he hangs out with. Once you can analyse these things, you will know why he is getting the results he gets. Sometimes, we become too busy, we forget to take out time, pause, check our activities, and question ourselves if we are really making progress. A lot of people confuse activities for progress, saying yes to quite a lot of things and are busy giving their time to everyone else except their dreams. **How do you grow a dream when you do not dedicate time, energy, and resource to it?**

Powerful millionaire habits.

One of the many significant habits of high flyers is their money habits. One thing is true -those you always find in lack, even after working for years lack money management skills. Here are some of the money habits of certain millionaires who built their wealth from the scratch. By this I mean millionaires whose wealth pegged between an average of over 3-9 million dollars, individuals and couples between the ages of 39-54 years.

Note: the results I will be sharing here are research-based carried out by a man named Faron Daugs, a personal financial planner who also doubles as the CEO of the company "Harrison Wallace". Having interviewed hundreds of millionaires, he came up with a summary of ten habits that were common to all of them in terms of their financial life. I feel it is important to share them with you because they are very valid and they show practical steps people took to become rich and stay rich. If you study them and you begin by adopting just one or two for starters, it will not be long before it begins to reflect in your life.

The millionaire habits

1. **They avert debt:** Contrary to what people think, people who are successful try as much as they can to avoid debts, and this is because borrowing comes with interest.

    The more you keep borrowing, there interest you get to pay, and as time goes by, even when you begin to earn more, and you have less to save because your debt interest is on the high side.

Does this means they do not borrow? Yes, they do. But when they do, they pay off as soon as possible, and they also do not take more than they can pay. When the rich borrow, they borrow below their means.

2. **They save for emergency:** If there is one stroke which hits everyone without prior notice, but asks that we prepare, it is the emergencies that come over time.

   Those with the millionaire foresight already have a plan to beat this monster, by saving. At least 10% of wherever revenue they get is diverted for emergency funds, which tackles the rainy days.

   Poor people eat all that enters their pocket-either wages, or stimulus or gifts- with the excuse that they do not have enough, but the truth earning more does not mean your problem margin gradually reduces. In fact, the more money gets into the bag, the more responsibilities you have to carry.

3. **They invest:** One rule you need to guide you through is that you can never become wealthy by working your ass out for money. If you try to do so, you will be broke, you will break down and that same money you work for will become hospital bills.

   The rich understand this and so look for several ways to make their money work for them. Study the stock markets, ask questions about bonds, forex and the likes, speak to an expert and find a way to put some of the said money into an investment plan for long term.

4. **Make this paper value get on its heels for you**, the surest strategy is by investing it. Now if you live on a small paycheck, your investment will be hinged on how much you make, but make sure you are putting aside at least 20% of your income for investment, emergencies, and retirement purposes.

   Moreover, your age should determine the level of risk you should take. Financial expert, Daugs, advises that when you are less than 30 and are planning for your retirement, it is advisable to take bigger risks as per investments, because you still have enough time, but the moment the 40s cross you, minor risks are advisable. Accordingly, if you are still lurking in your prime, what you have here is great news, that is another recourse to make the best out of your life.

5. **They do not follow trends:** Millionaires do not try to get rich to prove a point, they also are not bothered about the current fashion trends.

   People who understand financial freedom get things because they can afford them not because they are trending or trying to attract attention. In fact, when you find people who are moved by every glamorous thing in the fashion space, they are either spending money they did not work for or have poor finance management skills.

   This has caused a lot of people, who used to experience an abundance of money, to go broke, since they made a lot, but the issue explodes when you cannot grow what is made, ending up losing everything

6. **They take advantage of tax deduction:** As much as they can, people who are rich try to get tax breaks or tax reduction.

   They also look for more opportunities to pay less and get more for themselves, while others see it as selfish but Daugs sees it as being smart. The more you can save for yourself, the more you can multiply and invest.

   The more you participate in activities that are social growth-oriented, the more opportunities you have to pay less taxes.

7. **They have other streams of income:** It is never the best move, drawing all your income goals from one basket; it is a very dangerous thing to do and the long-term effect is disadvantageous.

   That is danger lurking around and when it comes knocking, it knocks down the door. This is the same reality the recent pandemic shuffled into many lives, since people were cut off supplies, companies went under, establishments that had stayed rooted for decades unexpectedly liquidated.

   Imagine what would happen to those who banked solely on these establishments only to be faced by a pandemic induced loss.

   It does not matter how much you earn; always look for ways to save money and, while saving, start studying and looking out for other viable sources you can put your money for fair returns. It does not have to be that much, since just a little drop daily is what makes an ocean.

8. **Early preparation for offspring:** A lot of parents are broke and needy today, not because they do not have money but because they simply could not watch their children suffer lack or want, so that they spent most of their earnings on them.

   People with millionaire mindsets however already know that having children is expected and so they begin to plan for it, even before marriage, some immediately after marriage.
   With this approach, they get to make the most of their own personal funds, while also catering for their children.

   According to Daug, it does not take much from you to begin, as the idea is everything follows the law of compound interest. They accumulate over time and it turns into something huge. How well are you planning for your kids?

9. **They are avid advice-seekers:** One of the world's best athlete, Sharq, was quoted once saying "greatest leaders are the ones who recognise and surround themselves with people who are smarter than them".

   When you find people who do not listen to advice or are arrogant, they are poor in character and may never become rich; if they found their way to wealth, one way or the other, they will not last long at that spot, before they fall.

If you want to be rich, you need to invest your time listening to people with higher ideas and perspectives on certain issues of interest. Being a professional in one thing does not make you a professional in others.

Therefore, to make decisions you need to depend on the ideas of other professionals, on your field of interest. Take advice, since it will save you a lot of money, energy and time.

10. **They take new cars over used cars all the time:** A millionaire would rather buy a new car and let it serve him for a long time than buying one that is already used.

    The time and energy that goes into servicing a car that is not new, due to multiple faults and breakdowns, would have been saved and extended to other things if one were using a new car.

    The issue with most people is that they would rather buy a big old car than buying a small new one. Therefore, they struggle daily and spend money they do not have, to maintain a car they do not need.

11. **They take every great option on the table**: Whenever companies want to offer you certain job positions, they often come with certain packages and opportunities that can help you save and invest, which is different from a retirement plan.

    Discover those packages and put them in progressive use

12. **Life insurance:** Employers in some organisations already have active life or disability insurance packages, which happens to be cheaper than trying to get it as an individual.

13. **Legal Services:** Most employers already have attorneys who prepare their legal documents, since they need to take advantage of the opportunity and utilise it, whenever you need to crate important documentation, like real estate, will and health insurance.

The habits shared here are what compounds to make people wealthy. Wealth does not just come; it is built by daily habits.

Money myths

Remember I talked earlier about how our minds have a critical role in the development of wealth or poverty; the things we hold on to shape our beliefs and our beliefs which begin to reflect in the way we act and respond to whatever is happening around us. I once had a friend who believed that if you do not spend what you have, more will not come, so he took his time to spend whatever money came into his hands. The effect was that he was always going broke and always in need. If someone at such a young age believing such a disempowering idea, it will be a huge challenge to build wealth, because all he cares about is eating everything he finds so that more can come.

This is the same way some people have adopted certain ideologies about money; how to make it, manage it, and multiply it. My job in this session is to open you up to some of the myths that have been doing harm to your finance and your financial growth. I will be sharing the most common and critical ones.

1. **I will do the savings later:** Research has shown that about one of every American neglects and procrastinates monthly savings. One of the biggest deception you will face as a young person is that voice telling you "there is still time", this is the king inspirer of all procrastination.

   Do not delay saving, that is your only guarantee for building something worthwhile. Even if you stumble upon any wealth, which I doubt can happen, you will still need the skills of savings to manage that money.

2. **My family deserves the best;** this mentality puts a lot of parents under pressure to try and meet the demands of getting the "best", making them spend a lot of unnecessary money they do not have. There is nothing wrong with taking your kids to a public school, while building wealth for the future; there is nothing wrong with wearing a cheap cloth, while making plans to buy expensive brands from investment yields.

   If you cannot afford certain things, at a certain point, due to long term plans, do not feel bad, as it is only for a while. Teach your kids to value money; show them the value of hard work and why they need to earn every penny that comes to them. With this, they will value even you more.

3. **I need to be rich to save:** Chances are that, if you do not save when you are broke, you will never save when you are rich. More money does not mean less problems, the more you get the more problems you try to solve.

   For example, if you had $10 with you, all you would think of is surviving, If that $10 turns into $100, you still think of surviving but you would have a choice on what you really want to eat. Once the $100 turns into $1000 it becomes food, few clothes, and maybe an apartment and this is how things change, our taste changes with income.

   Certainly, there is never a time money is laying somewhere, without thoughts of how to spend it crossing your mind.

4. **I need to be rich to invest:** There are billions of people roaming around the world right now with this mindset. I have had discussions with a few friends who would say "If only I could have this amount of money I could achieve this and that" so they linger and hold onto hope that one day something amazing will happen to them.

   Well, if hope or faith were the major determinants of how people experience success, I am sure a lot of people would have made it, but it is not. Finally, there is something I need you to practise whenever money comes into your hands, **always say to yourself "Not all of this money is mine, 20% of it is going into my future"** and the more you say this the more you begin to experience the need to save whenever money comes into your hands.

5. **Insurance is not for me:** I understand that a good number of people think insurance is not something they need, but you are not those people. You need insurance to take care of any losses you might incur in the future, and the burden will be removed from you and you would not have to stress.

   It is not easy giving money to insurance companies, but there are experiences you have no power to control and this is where insurance comes as a saving grace.

6. **Work harder and make more money:** If you think working harder will help you make wealth, you are mistaken. Working harder simply means trading more of your time for money while, on the contrary, your money is meant to work for you.

   Smart millionaires buy other people's time by investing; these people work for them trading their time, tasking in exchange a percentage of the revenue. Working harder may sometimes cause you to neglect your health, which may in the future affect your productivity or lifespan.

   Being smart is the game, since times have changed, the world is moving faster and if you must win, you must act smartly.

7. **Budgets are not my thing:** Not budgeting your spending automatically puts you in the position of being excessive; what really makes you rich is not just about how much you can make, it is about how much you can conserve, invest and multiply. The percentage

of your monthly savings will be judged by how much you spend daily. Accordingly, if you do not put your daily spending in check, what is left at the end of the month becomes less than you expect.

8. **High price means high quality:** Have you ever had an experience where you bought a product or experienced a service you paid a lot of money for, only to end up disappointed?

    A high price does not necessarily mean the product is the best. Sometimes, companies fly upon the wings of brand reputation to fix prices, which does not mean other options are bad, it is just the brand.
    Once you understand this, you will not judge quality by price.

9. **Buy, don't rent:** If you live in a place such as California where there is a neck cutting housing policy and killing tax, not to mention the homeowner's contributions, you will not adopt the idea choosing to buy a house over renting one.

These and more are some of the myths flying around as philosophies which some have even gone ahead to teach. If you found yourself in any of the following categories, take down that belief

Chapter two

Mastery Habits

How much do you know about those ahead?

Over time, I have dug into works of past experts, books and watched interview videos of people who have become successful. One question that is often asked is how their thought process works, that is, "what is it they have running through their minds always?" One common answer they all give is that they spend time focussing on what they really want and spend the other time figuring how to get them.

On the other hand, when you have discussion with people who are unsuccessful, what you find them commonly do, is thinking and talking about all the negative things happening around them, blaming other and pointing fingers, while spending most time thinking about what they do not want. The mind has its own unique way of operating and it cannot encrypt "don't"

The mind is focussed on words and emotions, and these words enact. For example, when you keep saying "I don't want to be poor, everyone else is poor, look at this broke and broken environment, I don't want to be associated with this dirty space" Your mind only sees poor, broke, dirty environment, and the emotions it creates often helps to keep you in that environment. However, when you focus on what you want and you keep thinking "I need to be rich, I need to leave this slum, I need to break the poverty chains in my family and become a person of influence" your mind creates and the next thing is beginning to look for how to get those things you want.

Several psychologists and from Maslow to Sigmund Freud have carried out research to figure out what causes the difference in the results people get during their lifetime. Why do some achieve happiness and others become sad, why do some people become very successful and others live a very poor life? They have one way or the other come to one single conclusion, which I will be sharing with you.

How we all grew up has a huge role to play in what we all get in life today. This phenomenon is called **self-concept**. Self-concept, in summary, simply means the programming of your mind based on the accumulation of all the thoughts, feelings, emotions, experience you have had all through your life, while growing up. It is more like the junction box of a house, where all the wires come together to create a system. This system now dictates the way we act, think and feel. Whatever level of effectiveness people experience from you is based on your self-concept. It is like getting a 240kjv generator into a system, which cannot produce more than has been imputed. It can produce less energy but not more.

This self-concept affects every area of your life, how you earn, how much you earn, what you invest, how far you can go with investment, houses and the type of houses you can build. It also affects your promotion and the level you can get in your professional ladder, It decides your ideas about work and improvement, determines your comfort zone, where you cannot stretch any further. For example, if all you have ever strived for was to earn $70,000 yearly, no matter what happens within or around you, recession, depression, economic meltdown or a boom in the economy, you will end up coming back to that level of $70,000.

The same thing goes for someone whose self-concept is pegged at $120,000, even if he or she loses his/her job, gets another job with less income, they would work their ass out to get back to that current level of $120,000 they used to be. The moment all the information about income you gave to your self-concept becomes registered, you will keep falling into that space.

Even if you go beyond it, by accident, promotion, luck or hard work, you will make a lot of crazy mistakes and fall back to where your mind is programmed to be. The only approach to change these results, improve your life, standards, income and influence is by working on your self-concept, until it is worked on and improved, your life will not improve. You need to change your thoughts about success, you need to engage your mind at another level of thinking, much more than what you have been experiencing before.

Some people see certain houses on the streets and the next thing that comes into their mind is "I do not think I can ever have enough to buy such a house, and, instantly, that takes a space in their minds, since the subconscious and the superconscious part of their brains immediately begin to work to make sure that what they have said comes into play. Consequently, whenever they see huge opportunities that can actually help them achieve what they saw years ago, they become scared or feel unprepared to take it; they feel they are not qualified.

Break that Self-imposed curse

Now that you are aware of how your self-concept is affecting the results you get from life, how you behave, feel or act, the next question becomes how do we eradicate that limiting factor and create something new. There are three ways through which this can be done and I need you to pay rapt attention to what I am about to share.

There are three different self-concepts that make us who we are. One is our *ideal self*. Ideal self-is about all that we see ourselves such as our dreams, hopes, vision, and possibilities we crave. This is mixed with all the values we see in ourselves and those we admire in other people.

Your ideal self-summarizes everything you see in yourself, whenever you want to define your future personality. Then, when you see people who are highly successful and are filled with happiness, these are people who have a very articulate idea of self.

Conscious of their desire, they are triple tasking to work them out. They have figured the right kind of people and role models to follow and they follow them; they have a clear picture of the values they need to emulate, and they emulate those values. When you stop a highflyer and ask what he/she thinks a successful person should be like, they do not speak as though they are unsure; they speak from a place of clarity and conviction.

Due to how the universe works, whatever you call forth in your imagination, thinking and action automatically comes to you; it may take time, but it will. The clearer you are about who exactly you want to become, the faster it is to become that person.

How much of successful people do you know?

When we were younger, we used to watch TV series of several superheroes, from superman to Batman and the likes. There is an internal surge of energy and motivation that builds up within us and makes us believe we are almost invisible. We imagine ourselves flying like superman, throwing webs like spider man and running after bad guys like the Batman; some of us, even in our dreams, saw ourselves saving the world. Very funny to reminisce today what our bigger dreams were all about then, the fantasies and the hopes that one day we would become superheroes.

The same rule applies today, in the making of great men. One of the most common qualities that all successful people have in common, based on their confessions, during interviews and in their books, is that they all have a story of studying the biographies and life stories of other successful people that have gone ahead of them. The more you read, watch and interview people to try to figure out how they became successful, the more impressions that knowledge makes on your actions, so that you simply find yourself trying to toll the same path.

Research has proven that people who surround themselves with great personalities are much more attuned to becoming like those same role models and the same happens with children who grow up in a negative environment or around negative people. This also affects people's self-ideals. When you ask people, who are living below the pyramid of success, what their ideal future personality is, they, unfortunately, cannot tell. They lack clarity in their articulation and cannot say for sure what they want from life. "The desire to be a person of substance" is not enough to define your future self, you have to say it in detail; how much you want to earn, what kind of family you want to raise, the values you need to have, your approach towards humans and business. All of these makes up the right idea of self-ideal.

What are your values?

Yes, it sounds basic, but it is critical in determining how people end up on life. When you can find the people, who have the kind of results you desire and you begin to follow the same set of values they emulate and display, your life begins to sharpen itself in the same pattern as theirs and your results are similar. It is basically about modelling another person's path, the result is that you will either get as far as they can or go farther. People who do not go far, have role models who did not go far, emulate the same set of values and get the same results as their predecessor(s).

Applicable in attracting resonating humans, the more you display certain values that are similar to success, the more you attract successful people. Your circle suddenly begins to change as your life changes, so that the results you get also follows through.

Who do you see in yourself?

When you take time to reflect and audit your life, who exactly do you see? Do you see a miserable, destitute hustler who is just trying to get by? A don in his/her specialty? Do you see yourself, as the best in your game or does your mind keep telling you that you are nothing?

Self-image is the second part of our thread on self-concept. What you see when you look at yourself determines your level of happiness, how productive you will become, and what is going to come out of your future. People who look at themselves and feel pity, talking about how unproductive and how unserious they have been, often get the same results.

That inner reflection of yourself and all the qualities that make up your personality, as you try to walk into that event, sit for that interview, speak with that the person you admire so much. If your image of yourself is not positive, it shows in the way you feel about yourself, and this goes ahead to reflect in your actions.

What to be done

You need to keep giving your mind pictures of the possibilities of your potential and begin to act in resonance with that image. Visualize yourself speaking at your best, performing with so much professionalism and excellence. Put yourself in the best league in your field and visualize them seated and listening to you share your ideas.

Do this consistently and, one day, the opportunity to highlight all of these rehearsals will come. Since you have practised and made your rehearsals a habit, it resonates and begins to replay those moments and you will do exactly what you saw yourself doing. The right words, actions, articulation, voice tone, and posture will find a way to give your best expression.

Self-esteem

We have talked about the ideal self, self-image and, finally, we need to talk about the third concept, which is our self-esteem. I know you have heard about this quite a lot, I will go a little bit deeper. This is a very vital part of your life and essence that controls how you feel about yourself, the energy you exhume, and your performance. The moment your self-esteem begins to reduce, things will not go down well. This is because we all do what we do to either improve our esteem, maintain it, or protect it.

Therefore, in trying to go around your daily activities, you need to understand that everything you do affects the way you feel about yourself. For example, you were at an event trying to celebrate, you were all over the roof, your old friends were present and you were all having fun, then suddenly you realize your trousers had a hole in them and your undies are there in public view, you suddenly lose that zeal, the energy reduces and you embarrassingly walk out.

You must do everything to make sure your esteem is not hurt, because if you allow people to disrespect you, insult, or make jest of you, it will be difficult to make the best out of your life. Respect is the game.

The Comparison game

There are times, whereby the core contributor to the low self-esteem people often feel, is self-comparison. People often compare where they are, present state to their ideal state. People become happier, whenever they see signs that they are living in a manner that is in line with whom they want to be, they want to do more. On the other hand, when you begin to notice that you are inconsistent with who you want to become, you feel bad, which is a problem of clarity. People who find themselves in this box do not have enough articulation about what they really want to be and who they want to be like, but you do.

Love yourself daily

This is one the greatest mind tricks to increase your self-esteem. The more you tell yourself how much you love yourself the more you do, whoever you love, you have more confidence in yourself.

So telling yourself "I love you" automatically increases your confidence in yourself. The more you operate in the area of your skill and do well, the more your motivation to do better increases, and, as it increases, you will do better, and gradually, it will begin to extend to other parts of your life.

Chapter Three

The value habits

The world we are in works basically on the principle of exchange. Whenever you want something, you have to give something in return, nothing comes for free. To take in oxygen, you need to first give out carbon dioxide, when you refuse and hold onto that carbon dioxide, you will not get any oxygen and you will eventually die.

If you go to the market today to ask for food, they expect you to bring money in exchange for the food you want. Except you are a beggar and want to be treated as one, you must take money to wherever you feel something, if value picks your interest, and this is how value works. If you must earn more and become wealthy, you must become not just a person of value but a person of high value. The world recognize, respect, and value people of value.

Never make money your reason

The year 1903 marked a remarkable moment in history, a

moment that was going to change the way the world operated, loved and experience life generally. Two men had just invented something that would become a whole new industry, somewhere in the United States, and later extended to the rest of the whole world.

Wilbur and Orville were brothers and children of a preacher and his wife, Milton Wright and Catherine. Whenever their father came back from his missionary journeys, he was used to buy them toys of different caliber, but, on this particular day, in 1878, he came back with this particular toy which made the boys so curious, and that curiosity was going to change the history of the world.

It was a medieval model of a helicopter created by a man named Alphonse Penaud, who was known to be the father of the Aeronautics. These boys would later drop out of school to chase this dream of crating something that would fly like birds in the sky.

Wilbur was known to be very bright and inquisitive. He spent most of his time studying and trying to get the best of his life by reading several books. His brother Orville was more of the business minded person who knew how to make great business decisions.

They would spend days repairing and designing their own brands of bicycles for sale, while spending the evening working on their new found hobby, a plane. They achieved their first feat in the year 1903 after flying the first airborne plane, a free controlled flight.

However, due to the general ideas and the crudeness of technology, it was predominant then that people still did not believe the appreciation was not coming forth, and these brothers knew they had to do something.

They moved in to Europe in 1978 and found that their theory and works were more appreciated there, so they stayed. In 1809 fame came, they got the recognition they deserved; they started a plane manufacturing company and became very rich. Nevertheless, beyond riches, these brothers are the reason for having an aviation industry today.

Why do you do what you do?

One of the strongest ways to try to work is because of money. The moment you make money, your motivation will not stop hustling and, when you hustle, you really cannot make a change on a large scale.

Never make money the reason you want to work, but attach purpose to what you do, which would give your work a different approach. Imagine if the Wright brothers were all about the money, of course someone else somewhere would have built the plane and they would have lost that opportunity of taking a place in history.

Do not try to make money; just try to become a person of value and money will automatically follow you.

There are levels to value

Even while I talk so hard about becoming a person of value, you must understand that there are levels to value. A gateman giving people access is of value but that value cannot be compared to that of the personal assistant, and the value a personal assistant provides can't be compared to those of the manager.

Therefore, in your journey towards becoming a really successful person, you need to learn to climb the ladder of value. If you offer solutions to ten persons maybe hundred will appreciate you, but if you offer to a thousand person a hundred thousand will appreciate you. If you want more respect don't try to make more money, grow and make impact on the lives of as many as you can, you will rise to another level automatically.

Invest in knowledge

Prior to when the first plane flew, the wright brothers had a history of following several engineers and their works. Certainly, they had a knack for engineering projects and were ardent followers of Otto Lilienthal, a German Aviator, whose death, during a glider ride, led them to begin their own journey into building planes.

Millionaires are not dumb people who put their faith in something that is not realistic, since they make decisions based on facts and data. They study trends and then align their conviction based on all the information they have gathered, and information cannot be available, except you open your eyes to accessible points.

Elon Musk was said to be reading about two books a day. He started his company SpaceX, a space transportation company, without any astrology.

He achieved this by reading a whole lot of books and speaking to a lot of smart people in the field. Today space X is worth over $100 billion according to Morgan Stanley. If you must be rich, you must invest a lot in knowledge.

The habits of value

We are all products of our thoughts and feelings, which then go ahead to determine how we behave at every point. This covers for 97% of what we are made of, our thoughts, feelings and behaviour, which are what makes our habits. However, they are learnable and that makes great news.

All of what you are today was learned either consciously or unconsciously. All you need is consistent practice for a particular period of time, so that a new habit is formed.

If you really want to be a person of great value, you must learn the habits of the millionaire minds. At the beginning of every session in college, we are sometimes introduced to new subjects, some building up the foundations we have already had while others are entirely new subjects, but one thing is certain, as we keep attending classes and practising both class activities and assignments, we begin to become better at that subject.

At some point, it becomes something we can teach someone else with ease. This is how habits come to be also just practice and repetition.

Good or bad habits?

One variation between good and bad habits is that good habits are harder to create but the reward is progressive, when experienced. Conversely, bad habits are very easy to form but the reward is destructive on the long run.

The origin of habits

We cannot keep talking about habits without trying to understand where they really originate. Psychology define habits as "one's conditioned response to stimuli". Take note of the word **condition.** This means we are all conditioned differently to act and respond to situations around us, this is why you find the rich reacting differently to certain things from the poor; this is the result of individual conditioning based on what has shaped our habits.

So habits are shaped by the peculiar way you react to certain things over time and, just as I have said, all habits are learned and they can also be unlearned. The question is now how?

Developing new habits

A pervolian Narrative

A psychologist called pavilion created an experiment, using a dog as a test subject. In that experiment, he placed a hungry dog in a room and then rang a bell, immediately the bell went off, he placed a meat inform of the dog.

He did this repeatedly and every single time the bell went off, he threw a meat at the dog. He noticed that every time the bell went off, the dog began to salivate in anticipation of his great meal, which happened even without the presence of a meat.

This is the same for humans too, since we have been so used to reacting to certain happenings that, even when the thought of that same thing comes into our mind, the emotions we feel every time it happens just springs up. This is because it has happened so much, and so our brain is conditioned to act that way.

Science has proven that the more you talk about the person you love to other people the more you love him/her.

The power of visualization

Have you noticed that whenever you are alone and you begin to imagine that the worst is going to come upon you or you feel something evil happening to someone close to you, you immediately begin to feel your heart rate go faster, you become restless and sometimes tears begin to flow from your eyes? Immediately you change your thoughts and begin to see the exciting things that could happen, the wedding bells of your siblings, the new car you bought, a contract, graduation or some new feat, your heartbeat increases this time but the emotions change into excitement, you feel the lightness in your chest and you feel good about what you could have become.

You see, our brain does not know the difference between real life and imaginations, since it works with the images and both the eyes on top of our head and the eyes of our mind feed it. But the one which comes from the eye of the mind is more powerful. That is why you have to use this power of visualization and consistently feed your mind with images of positive happenings daily.

When you look into the mind of the poor, they are always consistently feeding their mind with images of self-pity scenarios, always feeling sorry for themselves, and imagining that someday things are going to get worse. Accordingly, they begin to reflect on these thoughts. Rich people, even in season lack will not take what they see; they live up there in their minds, imagining how great their future will become.

Positive affirmations

Just as saying negative, keeps your life negative, saying positive, keeps your life on the positive increasing end. One of the daily rituals of millionaires is positive affirmations. This is one of the best ways to require the neurons in your brain to focus on only the things you want them to focus on.

There is a feeling that comes when you look at yourself in the mirror and speak about how amazing you are, and you begin to act that way all through the day. The reverse happens when you look at yourself and begin to talk about how miserable you are or have become, and walk through the day with a heavy heart.

I will be sharing with you some positive affirmations you can begin to practise today, and I can assure you, it is only a matter of time before you begin to see them reflect in your life.

Note that to get the best out of these affirmations, you will have to say them and be very serious about it, if possible, get emotional, visualize yourself becoming every single word that comes out of your mouth. Are you ready? Let us go

- I am in charge of my destiny, I will build my world, and my world will answer me

- I am full of joy, I am a joy generator, everyone around me is happy because of me.

- I have an intelligent mind, my soul is peaceful, and my body is healthy.

- I have multiple gifts, I am skilled.

- I have all it takes to change my world.

- I rise above every limit daily. I am filled with so much positivity.

- I am the most amazing being I have ever seen

- Wealth looks for me.
- Limitations have nothing on me
- I have a millionaire mind.
- Wisdom works for me
- I am a life learner, I am committed to learning
- I am a solution provider; the world looks out for me to provide solutions.
- I am a person of value
- I dedicate my time and resources to increase in value
- I won't stay in one position for long, I'll keep increasing
- Wisdom is available to me
- The universe avails to me everything I need to succeed
- I am a successful business person, I do the right business the right way.

Millionaire Affirmation:

- Money flows from me, through me, and in my direction
- I attract money
- I am free from all financial chains

- No burdens in my life.

- I have a millionaire mind

- My finances are exploding

Everything rolls around emotions

Emotions control everything we do. When you feel sad, your energy level reduces, you get a little bit depressed, things easily get you to react and immediately explode. But when you are excited, your energy level increases, you easily get along with others and can overlook people's mistakes. Visualising yourself as a millionaire, the best and greatest you have ever seen is one way to become full of the required energy it takes to win.

Emotions in habit formation

When it comes to developing new habits, emotions have a very great role to play, in fact, there are theories that have shown that the intensity of emotion you feel at a point determines how fast a habit is going to be formed. For example, take someone who has tried his/her possible best to quit sugar, sweet and anything that could damage his/her dentition but could not, then one day his/her dentist says: "Sir/Madam, if you do not put an end to candy consumption, we would have to remove these set of teeth in the next 5 months and the rest might become very painful to bear with time".

Immediately, the person imagines himself/herself without teeth, feeling the pain of tooth aching and before knowing it, someone who could not stop immediately ceases after an emotional encounter. This is known as the Significant Emotional Experience (SEE).

Experiences that shake up emotions such as sadness, pain or joy can easily create a new habit pattern one has been trying to create for a long time. For example, someone who drives really fast will easily quit fast driving, the moment a crash is experienced that almost took his/her life or put him/her on a death bed.

On another end, research has also proven that some new patterns such as reading daily, going to the gym, eating healthy, being punctual for meetings and the likes can be developed within 13-23 days by following a simple but powerful process. The more you repeat a process, the more it becomes stimulated, and you can use this process to create any pattern you want to create. Just the process of recurrence.

Steps to develop habits

Here are some simple but powerful steps you can take to start creating new patterns of habits. If you follow these steps, as I have stated, your habit formation process is maximized.

1. **Decide:** Everything we do begins with a decision. In addition, that is also the first step to creating a desired habit; once you have made your decision then you move to the second step.

2. **Do not condone self-excuse;** Let's say the new habit you want to form is going to the gym daily, the first two days will be hellish because you get to feel the pain effect from your mistakes and sometimes it's really difficult to raise up, so your body begins to suggest you stay down a little bit or stop. The moment

you begin to allow these ideas, you will see them gone. Do not allow exemptions, follow through with whatever you have to do until it becomes a monkish habit

3. **Relay your plans to others** When you tell people about your plans, they put you in check and try to see if you would pull through with what you have said. You also become accountable when you share your goals with others because you wouldn't want to look like a failure.

4. **Visualise yourself:** Once you have started, there are tendencies that people who know you begin to make jest if you; some would even swear that you cannot do it and would soon quit. These words, if allowed, can find a resting place in your mind and begin to mature. This is why you need to look at yourself daily and utilise the power of visualization. Allow your mind that desired state and let your emotions become attuned to what your goal looks like

5. **Affirm it daily:** Depending on the habit you want to form, find affirmations that relate with that habit and begin to use them. For example, if you want to reduce sugar intake, you can affirm that by saying "Today, I have lesser sugar in my system because it takes less sugar". As you do this, your brain becomes rewired gradually.

6. **Remain persistent:** keep going on, keep increasing your pace, and do not stop. Persistence increases the results you get over time and soon you'd be very proud of yourself. Also, persistence makes all those

who think you won't make the best of your life, when you started, respect you.

7. **Reward milestones:** There is a hormone in the brain, called dopamine, also popularly known as the feel good hormone: it is the hormone that is released, whenever we do something that makes us feel great, and it also aids the addiction to that thing. Therefore, every time you reward yourself for a well-done job, the dopamine chemical is released and you are inclined to keep doing the same thing.

Defeating procrastination

To be honest, there is no one in the world who does not deal with procrastination. We all get worked up to a point where our minds just begin to suggest to us about how we need to lay down and have some rest. Nevertheless, you have to overcome that thought because the moment you start entertaining it, the more you like being lazy and pulling off tasks.

The first step therefore is to make the decision not to permit it by starting with the things that are more important. Once you finish the first task, check off your to-do list, it immediately releases a dose of dopamine, which makes you feel well enough to carry out another task.

Secondly, do not give yourself excuses, tell others about how much you want to end being a procrastinator in that particular area of interest you have chosen and let them keep you accountable. Visualize yourself carrying out that task, and create enough energy to carry it out. Keep affirming, for example, "I will go to the gym for 40 minutes from 6am daily" then finally, reward yourself for every great work done.

One habit at a time

Sometimes the energy and adrenalin that rushes up our guts, whenever we learn about how easy it is to learn new habits daily, can cause some people to decide to start adopting and learning several habits and what that does over time, if it wears you out. If we focus so much on several habits, they all drain our energy and we form nothing.

In this case, what you can do is to choose just one habit per time, follow through with that habit until it becomes a subconscious action. When you notice this, you can then add another one to it.

You also have to be patient. The current habits you have formed and displayed did not take you one day to start, since they have been there for years so you cannot just suddenly rise up and try to change it immediately; your system would create a level of resistance. Do not sweat it, since you will yield with time.

A space for obsolete habits.

When you start learning a new habit, there is a tendency to think that the old has died, the truth's habits do not die: they only succumb to a new one due to our consistency in practising them.

They simply retire to your subconscious and try to pop up one time or the other, depending on how much you practise the new one. For example, if you learned how to drive a skateboard when you were younger, and as you grew up you began to drive cars, one day you picked up a skateboard after 15 years and before you knew it, in few seconds, you are already riding with the same level of skill you were riding before. All it took, for the same stimulus, to be reinstated.

Another example is the revolution of manual cars into automatic ones and now we have self-driven cars. As you begin to learn new habits of driving, the old ones from manual and automatic takes the back seat, but when situation demands you drive yourself, they immediately come back and take the wheel.

Convert your Anger

Rage sometimes can also work as a tool: there are several times it has been used by athletics to win matches. 50 cent in the book "hustle harder, hustle smarter" talked about a time Floyd Mayweather was to have a match with Conor McGregor. Prior to their boxing match, Conor had taunted, abused, and said quite a lot of crazy things about Mayweather but he never buzzed.

On the day of the match, 50 cents recalled he walked up to Mayweather before he entered the ring and whispered into his ears "This man is about to take food from the mouth of your family, what will you do about it?"

The reaction from Floyd was as though some powers descended and he entered into the ring with so much rage. The match ended with a TKO in the 9th round with Floyd Mayweather being victorious.

Anger when channelled through the right path can become a very useful tool for success. Rather than getting angry at everything and doing nothing about it, get angry and learn a skill, read that book, study and go for that exam. Take those classes, find a lasting solution to that problem and earn your place.

Chapter four

Business habits

As someone who is going to be successful and rack in millions in revenue, chances are you will spend a lot of your time dealing with the market. You would have to manage and run a business or several businesses.

A large population of millionaire in the United States of America are business owners who grew their businesses as first generations, that is, they started up with nothing to become millionaires. Therefore, learning and mastering the art and science of the business market place increases your chances of adding to the number of millionaires the world already has.

Having a successful business career does not just involve you dealing with the market places but with the people who make up these market places, the decision-makers from several walks of life, different beliefs, principles, values, ideology, and philosophies. So it takes more than just being a skilled business person to successfully sail with this set of people, since you need to develop relational qualities.

Why you are in business

There is a misconception most people have about the primary purpose of running a business. People think it has ruined more businesses than it has made, which is the misconception of "profit first".

In chapter three, I talked about you never making money your reason, instead of choosing to solve problems and money will come, this principle also applies in becoming a great business person. In business, your primary purpose is to bring value to people and keep those people glued to that value; if people love and stick with the value you bring to the table, money will not be an issue.

Do not make money your primary drive, if it does not come in the first few months, you should definitely pack up and leave that business. If you strive to create a business that would be a solution to the cravings of your customers, even if they do not see the value yet, you will not quit until you can prove it.

Satisfaction precedes growth: Customers are the ones who grow businesses, since businesses do not grow themselves. If you run a business that is not aimed at creating customer satisfaction, your business will be left for another person that can create and give the costumer something better. If your business must grow, you need to find a need, create an offer around that need and drive traffic into buying that need.

Clarity: Clarity is also another powerful tool for getting the best out of every business. Questions like "what problem exactly do we solve?" what is the vision for this business? what is our aim? need to be stated. It is easy to follow every single trend if you do not have a defined statement or set of statements that guide your business. This vision statement has to be clearly ingrained in the mind of everyone who is part of that business, because trying times will come, storms will arise and there are days when things gets hard and you want to throw in the towel, but the vision is what keeps you going, as an entrepreneur: it is what reminds you of why you started. All successful brands and companies have vision statements they follow.

Mission statement: According to Harvard Business School, mission is simply defined as the steps a company is going to take to take to achieve a vision. So, once the vision is articulated, the mission becomes the next step. One of the qualities of a mission is that it must be guided by milestones, something you can measure with time.

For example, a company's vision may be ***to help businesses achieve the growth they deserve*** while the mission may be, in other cases, to achieve this, we should make sure ***we put out our business strategy, marketing resources and expertise to study the market in relation to businesses and help business owners experience at least 40% increase in their revenues.***

If you have a vision and mission statement like this, all you will be doing will be guided by it, you will know what skill exactly you need to adopt, what resources you must find, what kind of people qualify for employment.

Define your "why"

A lot of people go into businesses without a why, no wonder they take anything, manipulate, get themselves involved in some gut-wrenching scandals and eventually go under. What crisis opened your eyes to this prevailing business? This has to be defined by you and you alone.

One Genius Vs. Many Smart brains

According to Collins, the author of "Good to great", after so many studies and research about the top fortune 500 companies of the world about their vision and mission, he noticed that those companies who grew to become great never hinged their vision on one genius; they brought many intelligent people to create the vision.

He likened this to one person in a bus trying to decide the direction in which the bus would go rather than everybody coming to decide where the bus should go before moving it. What if the genius was taking them to a wrong direction?

If you are trying to build a solo business with some level of revenue yearly, you can decide to choose and articulate the vision you want for that business, but the moment you want to build a company, something that would last long and outlive you, then you need more than your brain to decide where the business is going.

You need to surround yourself with many intelligent minds, who have some level of insight and expertise in certain areas. This is very important, because it is much easier for people to fight for a vision that they are part of than fight for another man's vision.

Goal settings, mapping

Having a vision and a mission is not enough, you need to break all of those big dreams and statements into obtainable goals that you can run with. For example, if your mission is to help business owners increase their output by at least 40%, then your goal can be:

- To create a business auditing course that can help businesses check where the problem of profitability lies in their business.

- To consult for at least five businesses.

- To organise staff training, in order to increase internal effectiveness and get the best out of these businesses. Short phase, extended phase, are all in your hands to draft.

Invest in marketing

The only way your solution can be known and patronised is when you put it out there. Without marketing, you are just blinking in the dark. You will have great products and services to offer but no one would patronise you.

What is marketing?

This is simply the art and science of communicating your product and services to the right audience. Take note of the words communicating and right audience.

One of the mistakes startups make is that they have a great product but try to market this product to the wrong audience, like "how do you sell snow to Eskimos?" This is what a whole lot of business people try to do, so they either end up not making any sales or not as much as they ought to.

In marketing, there are three major drivers of profit generation :

Message

Channel

Audience

Message

If you must sell something to someone, either an idea, or a product or services, it is quite important you craft your message in a format they can relate to.

If I cannot relate to your advertisement message, how do I become convinced that your product or service can help me solve my problem? For example, when coca cola wants to advertise coke in the USA, their approach towards passing the message is going to be very different from the way they advertise coke in somewhere like Nigeria.

There is difference in culture, language, beliefs, values, which are critical factors to be considered, before putting out their contents.

Channels

Auto mobile brands understand that they have no business trying to get to their audience through radio adverts, so they make use of TV and magazines. Social media application companies would rather make use of platforms like google, YouTube, and play store to advertise rather than past their banners on the streets or on buses.

After understanding who your audiences are, the next step is to find out where exactly they are and how to reach them. If you sell water, your audience is mostly in parks, malls, bus stops, and sport centres.

Once you can spot where they are, then you look for the right channel to reach them. You cannot target people to purchase water from you using social media, except you are selling in truck loads, but if not, you need to invest in a store close to where they are. That is your channel.

Another example is: if you are trying to sell digital products, you need to utilise digital channels to get these products to the right set of people. Also, people who are active online are the ones who are most likely to purchase an online product.

Audience

If you already have the right message or value and are passing it through the right audience, they two are just about 70% of everything you need to create a good business. You need to make sure the right people who want and can buy your product or services can see your adverts.

For example, if you are a real estate agent representing a top real estate firm, the least of your houses is about $700,000 and you want to make advertisement via Facebook, you definitely must not target college students or low income earners.

They will not buy and Facebook does not care who buys either, they expect that you have done your due diligence in figuring out the people you want to target and getting them to buy.

Another example is if someone is trying to sell sunshades and he/she is busy advertising on radio stations, the result is loss of labour and a waste of money. Glasses are best sold either on fashion magazines to appeal to people who are already fans of fashion or on the internet to those who carry out their activities around digital fashion blogs. Their ages too need to be put into consideration.

Think customer satisfaction

Your greatest assets as a business person is the first set of customers that patronises your business: these people will determine if you will get more customers on referral bases. Therefore, in order to make sure they come back again for repeat purchase, make sure they get the best satisfaction for everything they buy from you, not just through purchase but every process that gets to the purchase.

The conversation, manner of response, speed of response, how your treat clients, and how you make them feel. These factors are very important in building business, because your customers are the reason why your business will either fail or succeed. There is a common business quote, which says *"Customer is king"* and I accept that to be true.

No matter how great your brand appears to be; if you have poor customer service, you are gone.

You must know how your customers think

Almost all humans are ethically selfish when it comes to buying what we need. We practically want as much as we can get for the least price and we do not want any stress in the process of getting it too. It is your job to make sure you input this thinking onto your production and service process.

Since customers want something better than what they got yesterday, you have a responsibility to improve. Never get too used to selling a particular type of product that you forget: it is only a phase before people keep trying to look for something better. Once you cannot satisfy those urges, they will leave if someone else comes with something better, just like blackberry and android.

Blackberry had the opportunity to remain as the market king they were but failed to improve. Everything went down when they finally sold the most important and unique part of their phone, Blackberry messenger. The moment people saw they could have a BlackBerry messenger on an Android phone without having a BlackBerry phone, they immediately swapped and that was the end of BlackBerry.

Whether that business is yours or someone else is putting you in the position to manage it, your two biggest interests in improvement points are customer satisfaction and delivery.

Simple steps to win customers

You must have heard a popular business saying, "do not fall in love with your products, fall in love with your customers" now, that is a very true and authentic statement you need to live by as a business owner.

Your customers are the killers of revenue for your business and doing everything you can to keep them proud and loyal if very important. I will be sharing with you some simple and powerful ways you can get both prospects and customers to stay with you for a very long time (if not forever).

1. **Deliver on or before time**
   Once you can keep to delivering the orders of your customers and prospective customers before the said date or on the particular date you promised, their trust in your brand increases and there is an opening for repeat purchase. If you fail to deliver, that is the

end of that trust, and we both know the key part trust plays in any relationship.

2. **Treat them as humans**
   I have had the rare opportunity of experiencing and reading about companies, firms, eateries, and the likes, whose staff or the customer service unit treated a customer like trash and news went out, many of those brands never recovered from the effect of that.

   Do not count your customers like you are counting figures; you are actually dealing with a person with flesh, blood and emotions.

3. **Go beyond transactions, give them an experience**
   People may forget a product or service but they will never forget an experience. Sometimes, people even buy because of the experience they got from either the sales team, management, customer service, or the product itself.

   What is the experience behind that which you are trying to sell?

4. **Simplify your message**
   One of the reasons why a lot of companies do not have quite a lot of customer patronage, even when they have great offers, is because they complicate a lot of things.

   The human attention span is becoming lesser and lesser daily and people do not have all that time trying to decrypt a message.

   You need to make whatever you are offering as simple as possible so that anyone, at any level can understand. There are times I have visited websites of some start up brands and it is so obvious that they will definitely struggle to get paying clients.

Complex grammar construction, poor interphase, low quality designs and every other thing that makes up that experience. Give those details the scrutiny they deserve, that is how customer structures are created.

5. **It is better to do quality than cheap**
   If you reduce the quality of your offer because you want to make it cheap, it does not mean the people who buy it will praise you; if they ever get an opportunity to buy something of quality, they will not come to you. So rather than selling cheap and selling crap, raise the price to an affordable point, so that you can deliver quality. By this, you are not selling cheap, you are selling affordable products. For example, a cloth of quality goes for $200 in a known brand, but you can sell the same quality of cloths for $190 without taking a loss. It is better than selling a copy of low quality for $50 just because you want customer patronage. On a long run, this approach will affect your business and you will not be able to make as much as you ought to. Do not be the cheap person, be the person that is affordable and people will come running to you.
6. **Make things easier for them**
   Companies today are employing delivery systems to make things easier for their customers. People today would rather buy something that would cost them $1 more for delivery than leave their homes and spend over $3 trying to get it at the store for the same price. Even if the price of transportation to the store is the same as the delivery or a little bit higher, a lot of people who value time and want to relief themselves of stress will definitely take it. Make this your goal,

keep asking how you can make the life of your customers easier.

7. **Feedbacks for improvement**
   Never be scared to ask your customers for feedbacks on how their experience was with your products and services and how you can serve them better.

   This is in fact the best way to get improvement ideas, because it is not about you, it is about them. When someone or a group of people tell you that this is the way they want to be treated, this is the experience they want to have, whenever they come to your store, office or mall.

   When they realize that you implement those things, they love you and their respect and loyalty for your brand jumps immediately. Remember, it is what they desire, not what you want.

These seven golden principles will guide you to taking your route in the midst of the top companies in the world, if you work with them. Nevertheless, do not rush, you have to work with them gradually so do not try to do too much and loose the zeal.

You are different from your business

A lot of businesses crash today because the business owners have refused to allow the business run on its own, without personal interference and emotional impediment. A business is not a human even though it is run by one, a business does not have emotions, even when it is being run by an emotional being. A business is a system and should function like one. The moment you start choosing sentiments, brotherhood friendship, and affiliation over skill, expertise, track record it will spit you out.

When there is a need to make decisions, you need to make them to the interest of your business and its customers, not you or anyone else.

When the tides bring trouble, time will tell you it is time. You are an entrepreneur; you do not have time to start feeling bad. Once things do not work out, get indoors and device another plan, go out and project, keep doing that until you find the one which works.

Pivot when you need to

The biggest advantage small vessels have over the big ones is their ability to maneuver situation in the sea; this can be likened to small businesses and big corporations. While bigger corporations may find it difficult to initiate a change, smaller businesses can.

You need to know when to move, keep your mind open enough to know when a season is changing and begin to navigate new paths. If you refuse to change, others will replace you and you will lose out.

Another thing you need to invest in is in research. Research often gives you access to data to make decisions and also find new opportunities. Business will continue to grow when it continues to seize opportunities. Most small and medium-sized businesses that understand business restructuring well enough often have a department specifically designed for business development. The function of this department is to make in-depth research about its industry of interest, find out loopholes in that industry, create a tailored solution and develop a business model around it. With that, the company can work with several networks of opportunities, thus increasing its revenue on all sides.

If you must run a successful multimillion-dollar business, you need to employ the strategies I have listed; you have to make them your principles and guilds in that jungle industry of yours. Business has no emotions, business has no pity, it is a combat for survival and dominance, only those who have done due diligence dominate.

7 unavoidable habits you must deploy

Running a business is just the same as running your life; both are intertwined and demand some commitments from you. There are seven that you must adopt, if you really want to create a business that would stand out and, if you stand out, as a business person. These patterns are must-develop patterns; ignoring them will cost you a lot.

The first is organizing habits. If you must get anything done in life and your business, you must learn to plan. Without proper planning, you are preparing yourself for failure.

Planning time reduces execution time by a large percentage because you have a clear picture of what you want to do and you go straight to it. Research has shown that some Chinese companies create a plan for 150 years, most plans have been created to outlive even the founders.

Steve and Karen Anderson in their book, **"The Bezos letter"** talked about how Amazon's chief executive officer, Jeff Bezos since 1994 has written a yearly letter to staff, board members, and investors of Amazon about how each year went and the plans for the next one. Several, growing firms are known for having biannual or yearly retreats for the sake of planning the next year's events, happenings, and executions.

Planning itself revolves around asking very important questions and being able to answer them, while devising a plan to bring those answers to reality. For example, as a business owner or manager trying to navigate you need to ask questions like:

What do people need that I can provide?

Why do they need these things?

Is there anyone else providing these solutions to them?

If so, how can I do better?

What other benefits or extras can I add to what is already given?

Why don't some prospects patronise us?

How can we get them too?

What can we do better than our competitors?

Questions like these drive your brain into a deeper route of specificity. And you would be able to see new opportunities, faster than your peers.

You and your RAS

There is a system in every human's brain, whose function is to aid focus. This system is referred to as the Reticular Activating System.

Let me explain how this system works. If today, you decide you want to start learning about cars, the RAS takes up that command, and before you know it, everything about cars begins to get your attention. Even though you have been inside and/or around cars before, this time it will be different.

The system works on your decision to be more intentional; therefore, it begins to open you up to anything around that new intentional decision you have made.

It also works when you begin to plan for a day, by asking specific questions. The RAS begins to look for information around you that can help you answer those questions and, unlike before, you will be more aware this time. Get your Reticular Activating System to work by making specific decisions and asking specific questions and see how fast you would get results.

Arrange your plans

Now that you have your questions answered, you are fired up and you want to step out to execute well, it is not enough. You need to know the right set of people, tools, and resources that will help you bring your plans to reality. You need to arrange your plans to know who gets which position.

Knowing what things entail holds one angle of progress, knowing who to execute what holds another angle. If you know what to do and the right person is not there to help you do it, it is as good as not doing anything. Therefore, what is your plan, millionaire?

Delegate your weakness

Some entrepreneurs are very good at planning, others are great thinkers, and some are very good on the field, executing tasks, succeeding demands.

You know these people and what they are good at, so you can delegate responsibilities to them. You really do not have to play the one-man army; you will fail under scrutiny. Find people who can execute each task without issues and give it to them. In marketing, what the top executives do is to create content and that is it.

Every other task from setting up funnels, running advertisements, follow-ups, customer service are done by some other people. All they do daily is rising up and creating content.

Delegation does not mean you do not know what you want: it means you know what you want but are neither skilled enough to bring it to reality nor need time to focus on something else. Therefore, when you delegate, you must learn to monitor progress through proper inspection.

Inspection is different from micromanaging. Micromanaging means dictating what needs to be done by those whom you have trusted with a task without giving them the freedom to express their own creative ideas and expertise. As an entrepreneur, once you have delegated a task, the next step is to create a system where progress reports can get to you for analysis, questioning and suggestion or approval.

The right people make the right company

I believe you understand now that you do not need to surround yourself with people who will not be helpful to the destiny of your business, the ones who are can be a little bit of a task to find but when you do, you will be thankful for life.

Measure progress

If you really want to be very effective, you have to hinge your goals, plans, and execution on time frames and milestones, so that you know where exactly you are, as compared to where you started and how effective you are about time. Whoever is given an assignment, should be given with target numbers, and time frame for which those assignments must be completed.

Be open to everyone in the system

The position of your business at any time, in terms of revenue, losses, projects, and their status must be communicated to those who need to know at every point in time. Your board members should be able to confidently share about where the company is and where it is going with anyone.

Being open about information will go all long way in helping build trust, and create that show of transparency. People do not need to have to start assuming on something they could have easily got from the management, just because they were not open.

How to rule this business game

If you must win in the business world, you need to come in

with only one goal to win; if you are coming with any other goal, other than winning in mind, you will get less chances. They say, "Put the target for your flight on the stars; if you don't hit them, you have a place on the moon to fall back on, anyway, you are still above the multitude".

There are two types of teams in every league or competition you experience. The first team is the one doing everything to make sure they win; the other team is doing everything to make sure they will not lose. The first team will place winning as its benchmark and it will do everything it can to make sure it wins.

The second team is not necessarily interested in winning; it is not just interested in losing. The goal and ambitions each team holds will always find its expression in the way they play, each team's approach to the competition would definitely differ. One would go harder than the other and you can guess which. When you refuse to make winning the game your benchmark, you take everything else apart from the top.

I am here to show you some habits that you can adopt to win your business game and turn your company into a multi-million dollar company.

- **Never cease to learn**

    The biggest advantage businesses have over each other is what they know. Knowing more automatically gives you more. Never let knowledge be far from your bosom.

    Always put what you know to test and try to find new ways to do old things, the innovative approach you give to your business, the more it yields new results

and new results are what makes you stay relevant over time.
Never live by assumptions, especially if you run a business, since assumptions will kill your business and bury.

This is a space which deals with facts, data, figures and the likes, assuming what the market looks like, what it needs, how it operates and how to serve it is one of the biggest mistakes anyone can make. Invest on research, get external experts and let them give you insights on where your industry trend is moving and how you can navigate your business.

Also, never get to a point where you feel you can figure things out on your own, since you will be crushed. Top commercial banks have several consultants from different fields who consult for them yearly. Even with their top professional executives and managers, they still seek for external forces. **Why shouldn't you?**

- **Have a thought process**

    Henceforth, you must create a sieve every single thought or critical advice you go through, before taking actions.

    There are times you have to trust your intuition, but mostly, mistakes can cost you a lot, so you cannot afford to just rely on your guts. Some CEOs take ideas through the boards, then to the team of executives before implementing.

    Other smaller firms create an advisory system, which puts their ideas in check.

Sometimes, intentional delays can also assist you in helping you create the best decisions. Just because we are in a fast lane season, it does not mean all your decisions will be quick, since you have every right to ask for more time to think and reflect on whatever is presented to you.

No one should put you under the pressure to say or do something you do not feel you are ready for; your brain needs data to make correct decisions.

There are times where what is on ground requires that you have a thorough thought process and gathering of information through research, so as to make informed decisions. Opinions are made because they have data to support them.

- **Work with a closed group of experts**

There is a portion in the bible which states that iron sharpens iron. This means that if you desire to have that amazing continuous fire in the entrepreneurial world, while building your multi-million-dollar dream, you need to surround yourself with other amazing minds.

You are even advised to look for a group of people who are much smarter than you are. Being with them will continually challenge your mind, your thinking, shake and press down your assumptions, until you can find the truth. A lot of difficult business questions are also be easily solved with this set of people on your team.

So rather than spending hours, days, months trying to figure something out, you can do that, within a very short period amid other problems.

You can also join groups based on the kind of business questions they deal with. Accordingly, a team might be primarily focussed on just sales, while another could deal with business expansion.

Therefore, the predominant questions that hinge on your mind and business will determine the kind of conversations you will join.

However, I must warn you, being in places like this is not for you, to show off how much you know. If you live by this attitude, you will not learn anything, since you are there to listen and to learn. Until your opinion is needed, you are suggested to listen to everybody else.

With this approach, you will end up being filled with ideas, all the time.

Chapter five

Personal productivity habit

In basic physics, there are two types of energy: the potential energy and the kinetic energy. Potential energy is known to be the energy in static, while the kinetic energy is known to be the energy in motion.

Often, when an object is in a static state, it does not mean it does not possess energy, with the right amount of force it would transform and immediately begins to generate energy in motion. Man's purpose in this life is not to be in his potential state, he is meant for kinetic, stating all of what he can express while blessing the world with it.

Some people will leave this world without doing much, while others will leave their imprints in the heart of thousands and hundreds of thousands of years after their death. High flyers often give so much that they get to the top of their career ladder, create a better family, live a happier life, higher confidence, pride, self-esteem, and create legacies for their offspring.

On the other hand, you find people who refused to live their lives to their full potential experience a less happy life, stay at the average level of their careers, lower confidence and never really give their offspring something to hold on, as an aspiration. Be that kinetic energy.

What breeds high performance?

HABITS. That is what make those who perform high, and those who perform low. Their level of performance per time can be traced down to their daily patterns. It is not complicated or hard to discover, when you want to figure out how a man became successful; look at what he does on a daily basics and pattern your life after it.

This is good news, right?

Now guess what is better, it can be learned! All habits you find today did not come with humans when they were coming to this world, they learnt them and you too can. The only differentiating factor between people who get to start, maintain, and grow these habits and those who do not is discipline.

How disciplined you are will determine how much energy you want to put into learning a pattern you desire. Therefore, look around you, notice the people you admire and really love them and ask yourself, *"Can I do what it takes to get this result?"*

The personal plans

Yes, we have talked about how you can grow your business using some strategic plans and how those plans will give you amazing results, as feedbacks, but here we are looking at what these strategic plans will give you, if you were to personalise them. When businesses give you feedback in terms of revenue impact, your personal plans give you results based on energy and life expectancy. There is nothing as interesting as seeing efficient returns on the amount of invested energy (mental, emotional, intellectual, physical) you have invested in your life, which is the aim of this section.

My goal here is to show you how to pattern your life in a way that will generate amazing results, which will make you experience the type of income, growth, happiness and joy you truly deserve. These ideas, strategies and tools will set you on the kinetic motion, crushing every mediocre status in your life and helping you give your best to the world out there.

One of the top seven pattern you must develop is the pattern of daily planning, which is very important for you to get long-term results. One mistake a lot of people make is that they focus so much on the future results, neglecting what they need to do on daily basics.

Your daily routine is what compounds to make what you, who you are later, if you can seize your days on daily basis, becoming successful, on the long run, would not be a challenge. Give time to deep thoughts, visualise how you want your day to go, which steps and actions you will take to make it a reality before setting out. When your orientation is directed, your focus becomes laser beamed.

Short term planning, long term thinking

If I want to build a house today, before the foundation is laid, there are several things I ought to have done. First, the architect must have designed the house and interpreted everything to me in a way that I understand. The cost of calculations and estimation must have been made and soil test must have been carried out. Planning works the same way. The clearer you are about what you want to build, the more you become clear about what needs to be done today. I know how many bags of cement I need to buy, if I want to build a mansion, I know how many bricklayers, builders, engineers, electricians I need to get the job done if I were to hire today.

Short term planning gives you all the data you need to accumulate if you must achieve that long-term goal. Although the process can change, we might have to get more bags of cement, our water supply may get spoilt when we least expected, some builders may fall sick and get the project delayed, contrary to what we expected, but the goal still remains that we are building a mansion.

The journey might take a different turn, but the destination is the same.

Daily Editing

As you scheme every single thing you want to do per time, by writing them down, you also need to revamp them daily. Write and rewrite your goals of that particular day, as you have already achieved them.

Let us say "I studied for 60 minutes, I got the new mop and cleaned my whole room". Your brain automatically sends that message to your subconscious and the whole of your consciousness begins to work in that direction.

You become more energised to eventually get those things done. Everything you practise consistently follows you and eventually becomes buried in you and, before you know it, you begin to experience some sort of slow transformation, accumulating something of large effect. You, with less time, obtain better outcomes and fulfil more productive roles compared to your peers.

Journal

Because the thoughts come from your head, it does not mean they will stay. There are millions of ideas, options, insights, tickle that run through our minds daily and if you do not learn to write them down, you will keep losing track of the important ones.

Putting aside a template, book, diary, or note is a promising way to keep track of the relevant things you ruminate on, and the exact things you are going to take action on. I learned something significant about reading, when I was at school. Whenever I was reading, I kept a note beside me, where I wrote down the keywords and my insights.

Thanks to this method, I was not just able to get what I was reading, I could visualise it, smell it, feel it. My studies were on a deeper level because I was going for details then. If you must squeeze the juice out of your destiny, do what people who have the juice do. Take a book and pour out your thoughts every day.

Create your table

Another productive habit you can deploy to get desired outcomes is the habit of creating your daily table of what you want to do, in order of their importance. It can also be called a "To-Do list". When you have something that guides your daily living and the action that comes with it, you will know how to manage yourself to beat time. Time is not a quantity you can save, since it moves and does not bend or wait. However, you can prepare yourself and your day to maximise time and get the best out of it.

I see people who move around like fish, without a clear path of where they want to be at certain times of the day. These are people who get random calls from friends who want to see them and they drop whatever they are doing to answer; do not be like those people. You need to value your time so much that random things and people do not just jump into your life and steal it away from you.

The pareto rule

There was a socio-economist who proposed a law in the year 1985, whose name is Vilfredo Pareto and the name of the rule he proposed was called the 80/20 rule, popularly known today as "The pareto principle". This principle has been tested in all walks of life, in politics, law, economics, engineering, and it has proven to be true.

The pareto principle says that every 80% value you get from anything is always determined by the 20% of what you put into it. 80% of the grades you get from an exam will be judged by 20% effort you put into it. This means, in every 10 hours for example, that if you dedicate two hours to studying that course or subject you can understand 80% of everything you study at that point.

In business, this means, 20% of your buyers will contribute 80% of the revenue you will get per time, and 80% of the growth you will experience will be determined by just 20% of your patronising clients.

You need to focus on only the things that are most important in terms of results and value, and put most of your energy in them. What a lot of companies do sometimes is to figure out those clients which give them the best revenue and give them the best preference. If you can focus on that for your business, it becomes more profitable, you would not stress to grow and expansion comes with more revenue.

Mastering your top skills

If you really want to set your revenue on fire, stop trying to do everything or most of the things. After a critical self-evaluation, you should be able to identify your top two to three skills and the secondary skills. The task your top two to three skills require you to do is what you need to focus on while other secondary tasks needs to be given to someone else.

If you do this, you will see your productivity will increase, stress level will reduce and your income project will increase. This is how the cosmos awards you with more life. Trying to be everywhere will only cause damage to your health and when wellness is affected, productivity, peace and happiness reduces.

Control what you have power over

There are certain things that you and you alone can pull off, others that can be done by you, but they can also be done by other people; you need to find a way to relay those things to them. If you do this, it gives you more opportunity to explore your own skills at a deeper level of creativity. The more creative and insightful you are about it, the more other people begin to experience you, as a master in that field; mastering that field increases your respect in the industry, more money comes, you live a better life and you still have more time available for your family and leisure.

The moment I started taking charge of the things that I can control with some level of merit, I dropped others with people I felt were capable and my life changed.

A man can be very good at learning close to ten things and become skillful, become an expert in three, but he will only be recognised for one. Your task is to find that one you are sure to do better than anything else and focus your energy on.

Certain questions can quickly help you pick out the things you can do and those you can put out to someone else, you can ask:

>Do these things have to be done?

>Do I have other options; which are they?

>Do I have someone else with the same level of expertise that can deliver my expectations?

Do not leave it halfway

There is a lot of deep energy that goes into concluding a job. Every job you are set to do takes you through three phases before you get to the endpoint.

The first phase is where you begin to get ready for the job, the second phase is where you get into some deeper level to start pulling off the job, and the final stage is when you finally get the job done.

If you, for any reason, got yourself distracted at the concentration phase of whatever job is on your hand, you would have to start from the beginning again, by focusing and losing time and energy.

Learn to put your heart on the things you are doing per time and until you have pulled them off; it is not time to take any external distractions.

Whatever steals your time and does not contribute to your life is not something you want to pay your attention to, during work.

A ritual for your productivity

I am aware that you already have loads of ideas, strategies, and templates you want to follow to become more productive, and it can be crazy to start thinking of where to begin and how to get things started.

Do not worry, I have some practices that you can adopt which will break the complex chains of these tasks and give you the desired outcome in no time.

Firstly, you need to decide to put in a long time comparison with your colleagues. The more time you spend on that task, the more the habits of productivity become ingrained in you.

The moment the gun goes off in your head, just keep getting every task on your table done, do everything you have on your list to do, and see how your productivity will shoot up.

The bits and bits of daily delays in closing time, early resumption, and total disregard for every form of distraction is what compounds to make all the geniuses you find in offices, workplaces, industries, and the likes.

Secondly, the assumption here is you have already started doing amazingly well in managing yourself and getting the job done, but, this time, plan to get the job done, using a shorter period. Focus on how you can make the best use of the smallest allocation of time and see how you would begin to operate more efficiently. There is something the feeling of urgency does to your mind, when you get into that race and you need to get to the deadline faster than every other person.

Thirdly, be that person who knows to do whatever you are asked to do in a time less than what was stipulated. Never be found carrying out your job only when you feel like it, be known for executing the tasks on your table with a time lesser than what is expected. This sure path proves legit in stealing your superior's interest, increasing your workplace respect, and getting more on that paycheck.

Finally, just as I have shared from the other pages of this book, there is a tendency for you to get distracted with the feeling that the job at hand is the job that needs to be done because you did not put them on the scale of preference. You need to make sure that what is on your table per time is what needs to be on your table.

What you are doing at the time should be what you should be doing at that time, season, or stage, and anything else must be of lesser value.

You must understand that, if you keep putting all of your energy to execute those things, which are of lesser importance, they will not take you up the ladder. You will get them done excellently, but they are just what they are, unimportant.

1. **Only, get jobs you can execute excellently**

   You need to avoid the mistake of settling or taking jobs you cannot execute excellently; it will ruin a lot for you and the feedbacks will hurt you emotionally.

   If you want to get more tasks done with less mistakes, focus on the tasks you can execute with so much dexterity. The further you direct your gaze at them, the better you can execute others closer to them.

   Science has revealed that, whenever you carry out tasks in order of similarity, it becomes much easier for you to become effective, faster, and better.

   For example, if your most important task of the day is writing a four-page memo and you get it done, your next task between sending a broadcast message and reading emails should be sending broadcast.

   This is because it is a task closer to writing and the moment you are done writing a memo, it is much easier to step into a broadcast mode.

   It is a curve that is often adopted by many productive people. You will realise that if you follow this pattern, the more similar jobs you off, the less time it would require to pull off other similar jobs.

2. Choose one thing and get better

There is a ripple effect of choosing one thing and becoming so good at it on every other aspect of your life.

The more you try to become better at doing one thing, the more that thought begins to affect other parts of your life. Consequently, rather than trying to spread your energy and focusing on several things, choose one and master it, continuously becoming bigger and better at it.

For example, if you want to learn how to play a video game, the first time you try, do not last long before they shoot you off. The second time you try again, you last a little bit longer. The third time you say to yourself "Okay, I think I figure this out".

They shoot you down again, but this time, a little longer than before, you will try and try again, until you spend a lot of time playing this same game, which could not even last for 20 seconds when you started.

Dig deeper with the intention to discover and you will. It is the strict rule. This is how skills work; this is how you develop talents. Mastery is in repetition, mastery is in continuous learning

3. Prepare before you go in

No matter how great you think you are, never make the mistake of not putting whatever you want to say into practice before you go into that meeting, interview, or pitching session.

People can sense when you have done due diligence to research and carry out your own work; do not neglect that. If you must leave an impression that you are the right person in the room, you need to do some things right, creating time to rehearse before you step into that spot.

No matter how cliché it seems! College often teaches that no student fails what he or she extensively prepares for. If you study the way you ought to, you will pass the way you ought to. I have always seen results, as feedbacks, for whatever input you have made in terms of study and preparations.

If the score was 40% be sure you probably did prepare at an average level, and if the score went as high as 80% it also shows the level of commitment you have made towards being the best in that course.

Preparing gives you that respect you desire, which draws attention to you, so that people are impressed by your delivery.

There is a story about two heirs in a kingdom where an annual heir race was organised and the fastest heir got a huge reward from the king. A particular heir happened to have consistently won the huge prize every single time he seemed unbeaten.

Many tried but to defeat him but could not. Each year, he grew stronger and faster and every passing year beat the previous one, but something happened. He got so used to winning that he stopped whatever daily rituals he was involved in.

He would boast about how fast he had become he did not need to practise anymore; he could even close his eyes and get to the finish line. That same year, a smaller heir beat him to the race.

What happened?

While he was busy resting and bragging about all he had become, the other heir was working his body off, he was determined to win and he did.

It is not true that you have reached a point where you will not need training anymore, since the idea of static expertise is false. Stay in motion with your improvement, stay consistent, which is how you beat yesterday's feats.

4. Always keep to time

There are less than 6% of people in this world who are always early to wherever they need to be, and those people are not always difficult to figure out. Punctuality is one habit you need to also develop if you want to get the best out of life.

People perceive you to be more valuable, trusting that when responsibility is given to you, you will be able to carry it out, without hesitation. The more time you give to a thing, the more that thing becomes a part of you.

You do not have to decide to be early every day, just decide to be early each day at a time.

Being punctual makes it look like you are jobless and do not have things to do because everybody else comes late, but the truth is everybody else sees you and respects you more.

You may not know, but over time, the reward will come.

5. Fish out your limitation

Whenever you write down the things you want to achieve in your life or business either for the short term or long term, always try to determine the things or factors that may serve as limiting factors to achieving that goal, since dividing means to eliminate them.

For example, if you desire to dedicate four hours daily to deep study and research, you have to figure out the elements of distraction that will pose as viable threats to completing that objective. However, for this context, your mobile device may be the villain.

You can decide to set it off or freeze the applications on it, so that you can focus on other things. Once you can identify those threats beforehand and adopt strategies to eliminate them, you will get more done within the expected time.

If you run an automobile mechanic shop, first you must agree that people bringing their car is not the problem, thinking they will only bring their car when it is faulty, the problem would be how often they will bring their cars for repair.

You have no power over when they bring their cars, but you can determine if they will bring their cars over and over again by doing a great job. Even with poor marketing, excellent services can pull crowds into any business.

6. Edit your thoughts on the concept of time

One thing I have come to realize is that the more you become productive, the more you realise time is never enough and you need to do all you can to save more.

When I was younger, there were times I used to just sleep off and hope that time would just roll away, so that I could experience a season of bliss, like holidays, Halloween, and all. Nevertheless, as I got older and wiser, I began to realise how precious every single second is and why I need to save it.

What is your dominant thought about time?

Do you spend it judiciously, or you just allow things and people steal them whenever they want?

Whatever it is, you think will eventually have a reflection in the way you operate and the outcome you will find.

Make it a point of duty to learn about how to become more effective daily, learn and read articles about time management, look for better techniques, listen to podcasts or register for courses around that topic, at least once in six months.

The more perspectives you find, the better you become at organising yourself.

Get an accountability partner.

Squeeze out every single plunge of ripe juice I have communicated here and share it with someone else. Tell them about your plans, and ask them to keep you in check.

If you stay consistent, they let you know, if you do not, you will pay a fine to them. This will put you in a more serious mode, knowing that your integrity and money is at stake.

Chapter six

People's Skill

Quite a while lots of what you get in this world comes from other people. If you were to check everything you have now, around you and within you, you would realise they were all influenced by others.

Your salary was paid by someone, the T-shirt you have on got sold to you by someone else, the ingredients of the drink in your fridge, even the ones you made yourself, were sold to you. Your glasses, books, degree, your thoughts, were made by someone else; even this book was written for you to read it up to this point, which shows you are interested in what is written here.

This is why you need to learn how to roll with other people, because much of the emotions you feel will come from them. How much opportunities you will get, will be dependent on the people around and what they think of you.

I laugh when people talk about how they do not need anyone and cannot depend on anybody but go ahead to take public buses, trains and planes. Undoubtedly, the drivers and pilots of these systems just helped you by making sure you get to wherever you are going safely. We are all social animals, as Aristotle puts it; we were made for each other not to be okay on our own. Trying to push everyone aside, shows that something is wrong.

A lot of what you will feel within you, will be controlled by the people revolving around you and what they do. Therefore, you need to make sure you protect the core of your own essence, so that you can express it and resonate with those who match that same level of energy.

You must be consciously involved in only the things that give you peace of mind, because everybody else is, and, sometimes, what makes other people happy makes you mad, and so you have to put your happiness first before anyone else's.

Giving what is within

Unhappy people are often seen making others unhappy too. Some may try to fake it to the public by actually acting happily and making others feel the same way, but, if you really get close to them, you can see the lies in their eyes. What you do not have, you cannot give. If you must experience gladness, only let happy people in, whatsoever gives you less than that feeling ought to be locked out.

Make others feel great

There is a story of two young men who were rushed to the emergency ward of a hospital after a critical accident; they were both placed in the same ward, with their beds side by side. One had his bed close to the single window in their corner, while the other one just had his bed beside a barrier. They both got conscious days later and started bonding with low-voiced conversations. Over time, they got to know about each other's families, businesses, challenges, and success.

Due to one's inability to see what is outside the walls of the ward, the other one picked up the responsibility of sharing about whatever his eyes could see, whenever he got up from his bed. He would spend time describing nature, people moving around, lovers locking hands, motorist commuting. As he did so, the only thing the other man could do was just closing his eyes and visualise all that was being described.

Unfortunately, the first man beside the window got worse and died, and his new friend grieved and felt bitter for some time, after which he requested that the nurses changed his position so that he could also have an experience of the outer world.

The nurse understood his bid and took him to his desired position, that is the spot he badly longed for. Though in pain, he tried his best to drag himself up from behind so that he could see for himself. But a shock hit him: there was no window!

"What?" he thought to himself, what has my friend been describing then?

In his curiosity, he turned to the nurse and asked: "did you just put a wall here?"

"No", the nurse replied.

"But my friend spent the last few days describing what was happening out there to me"; "Oh wow", she responded with a mild smile "he was blind actually; he probably wanted to make you happy".

This is your first job in relating to people as those who try to build something significant. Being wanted, appreciated, loved, and accepted, would go a long way in the judgment of who you are.

No matter how skilled you have become in an area, once people do not like you, and they are in the position to place you on higher grounds, they may never recommend you. Humans are controlled by emotions, since we are emotional beings, and how we feel about people matters. You need to take that part seriously, once you know this, you will relate better.

Just as people react with emotions the way you create them, you also react similarly and respond whenever someone also treats you in a way that pricks your emotions. If you understand this, then you should know how to find your way around people. Positive attitude brings positive responses.

Therefore, you need to learn how to put all your elements on communications into making sure people feel the respect they desire. Say something about them, what they do, their family, if present. If they came to you or you met them with their spouse, appreciate them, tell them how awesome their spouse is. This could water the ground and with a little push, you can have your way.

People do not hire, buy from, recommend, or invite people they do not like. Accordingly, you have to be likable, which is a pattern you have to consciously cultivate. Once you can, doors automatically start opening for you, promotions come without stress, and people will speak for you within the corridors of power.

You also experience the reverse, when you do the reverse. Whenever you do something to hurt the feelings of people, you downgrade how they feel about themselves, and it comes around to affect you too. Just as I said before, a white light will not give out green light. Making others feel like they are nothing is a strong sign that you may also be nothing.

Whenever people tell you that they want to be loved, respected, and talked to in a particular way, please do as they say because that is the only way to win their hearts. Additionally, when they tell you they do not like being treated in a particular way, also take it in good faith and do not try to make them feel that way.

Respect me tag

Everyone -adults, kids, mothers, teenagers, youths- every single human with flesh and feelings walks around with an invisible tag on his/her head saying "please, respect me". No matter how small people look, as long as they have emotions and they feel pain, the moment you disrespect them, they feel it and that feeling rarely leaves them. Therefore, this habit is one you have to pay a lot of attention to, because it goes a long way to inscribe your profile in the hearts of those you find on daily basis.

You cannot change people's minds.

After the Iraqi invasion by the United States military in 2001, a lot happened. There were bombings here and there, attacks, missions upon missions went on, and several face-offs between the United States military and the Taliban locals; it was hard to watch how a lot of people reportedly died. There were casualties from both ends and the United States Army in the bid to restore peace and trust decided to launch an operation called the operation's hearts and minds.

The idea was that if they needed to win against the terrorists within those local spaces, they needed help from the natives, but if the natives did not trust you, and hated you, how could they willingly give you information.

So they thought about starting this campaign primarily focussed on developing social structures, providing social amenities, such as water, food, education, and support for the chiefs.

Until people begin to see you as someone they can trust, it is difficult for you to get them to change their reasoning over certain issues. There are times, as you grow in business, you might have to discuss with someone in a position to change or alter something in your favour.

How do you do that, when they do not have you in their heart?

One of the many paths you need to dig in your interaction with people is the path to their hearts. Once their heart is won over, you can get them to change their minds on certain issues.

The Four fundamental questions

In order to keep yourself and your actions in check, there are four recommended questions I think you need to fix in your heart and consistently ponder on.

The first question is *"**what would be the outcome of our world if every human being were like me?**"*

If after a critical analysis, you cannot acquaint yourself, you will have lots of work to do. People who fail to provide the right answers are the reasons why we have a messed-up world.

"What would be the outcome of this country, if everyone were to respond to both internal and external situations like me?"

This is another angle to show the true reflection of your character as a citizen and a nation builder. If everyone chooses to be like you, would crime, fraud, alcoholism, violence be eliminated or would we just have a system collapsing on all sides?

Now look at your company and ask the same question.

"What would the contents of my company look like, if everyone took on my behaviour and acted the same way I do?"

Would there be a more compassionate staff, are people going to help one another better and not try to pull each other down? Will there be harmony and teamwork or will chaos spread like wildfire. Does my company really need someone like me in the helm of affairs?

The final question goes to your family, *"what would your family look like if everyone treated each other just like you?"*

Do you think your family would become better, happier, and more progressive? These questions often take us to a default state, to think about life from our qualities and values.

When you take out time to consistently throw these questions at yourself and reflect on them, they help you shape a better man, and by becoming a better person, everything around you is influenced to automatically become better.

Ideas for better relationships

1. **Listen more**:

    one thing you should notice is everybody likes talking about himselves/herself; people always want to be the centre of attraction on wherever you are and in whatever conversation they are involved in.

    If everyone is trying to share, it is important to pause and listen. Once you can master the art of listening, people will automatically click with you because they always want to talk, and you are always there to listen.

    To develop this habit, first you must have a resolution to be the best person anyone can confidently speak to, because you listen. Secondly, pay attention to listening attentively, whenever someone is trying to share whatever information with you.

    Thirdly, do not stop until people start talking about your listening skills.

2. **When asking, practise reverberation:**

    When people are talking, one way to get them to see that you are listening attentively is that you ask direct questions.

    Try to start your question with what they said while they were talking, using statements like "If I understood you clearly, you said..." then go ahead to ask your question.

When people sense that you did listen, they want to share more with you.

3. **Practise gratitude:**

You need to practise gratitude by starting with yourself.

What are you grateful for?

Is health, life, growth, family the happiness you experience daily?

A thankful attitude for the things you experience automatically brings you into a deeper experience. Some people choose to complain about everything bad: all they see is the mold in another man's eye.

You are the one with positive energy, you are not a whiner, and you are filled with gratitude. Also, you need to extend this art of gratitude to other people. You must learn to appreciate everyone who is playing a positive role, no matter how small it is.

Learn to tell them thank you, even when they feel they least or do not even deserve it.

4. **Learn to compliment:**

Whenever people buy something, a cloth, shoe, tie, bag, or what you have, they buy due to the emotional connection they have with that thing. Accordingly, when they put them on, and someone compliments them, they get so excited, even when they do not show it.

Their confidence increases, how they feel about themselves boosts as well. Make a habit of pinpointing the intangible qualities people possess in appreciation like punctuality, diligence, loyalty, small and huge achievements.

Tell people about how inspired you are, about how far they have gone, share with them how much you appreciate them for their business, how well they have built their company, and sustained its growth.

Compliment people's wives, children, and workers. In that public space, tell the waiter "thank you". They will smile, they will become happier and you will also experience the resonating effect.

5. Help others build their self-esteem:

We all desire to get praises and appreciation from others, but the real deal here is who will praise and appreciate others?

You need to learn the habit of appreciating other people, whenever they do something worth appreciating. To make it even better, appreciate them in front of other people, tell people how great they are and express those thoughts with Genuity.

When you do this, how they feel about themselves takes a positive turn, self-esteem increases and they put that good they earned praising in the first place on repeat.

When you see videos of dog trainers during their training sessions, you notice whenever they want their dogs to do anything, they simply make them do it, by offering them a treat. These dogs, being aware that flowing commands would earn them a treat, continue to carry out those tasks, whenever they are ordered, which is called the positive reinforcement strategy; the ability to appreciate someone for something so that they can keep up with it and even look for ways to do better.

Praise rules

When you are trying to appreciate people for jobs they have performed, you need to be careful in order not to step on the ego of others, insult others or overflow the trumpet of whosoever you have chosen to praise.

- You need to make sure whoever you are, appreciating is being appreciated, as soon as possible, not later when the impact of what they did is less felt. If someone does a good job and everyone is there present, appreciate him right there.

- Do not appreciate them only for what they did then, do not beat around the bush, wherever it is they have done specifically is what you should talk about. This would make them see where exactly they have done a great job and put more focus there next time.

- The better they do, the more you need to tell it to them. Never stop talking about how proud you are; say it consistently so that whatever they are doing right, they start looking for more ways to improve.

    For example, if you have someone within your staff who sends reports on time or earlier than stipulated, never fail to always say how much you appreciate their punctuality and whenever they do not make it or send the reports late, do not complain, but ignore it until they do it right again.

This would immediately send a message to them that they really need to make sure reports are done and sent on time so that they can get recognised and appreciated. Keep a great behaviour great, by pointing it out and celebrating the person who expresses it.

Do not assume you understand

When people are trying to share something and you do not quite get the details to a point that you are sure you understand what they are saying, do not proceed with the assumption that you do make your scrutiny direct *"sorry, I couldn't comprehend your previous statement. Do you mind sharing again?"* Questioning is the way you own a conversation, if you can ask the right kind of questions you will easily find answers.

Make that conversation yours.

If you want to deploy a professional approach towards having a great conversation, you must learn to ask questions. It shows you are not trying to lose details and you are very concerned about the progression of the conversation. *"What exactly do you mean by that?", "I'm not sure I understand what you just said"* Asking questions like this brings the speaker to share more details and, with more details, you drive into clarity faster.

That is the way professionals differ from random listeners

Summarising, one of the strongest advantages you have in every conversation is in your ability to own that conversation.

You do this by making sure you ask direct questions, pay attention to their feedback, do not assume understanding, and never rush to give your comment.

What truly matters?

Let us quickly start a question and answer session, which is the same query I often make from people, whenever we try to sort out issues regarding how to become more effective.

I would implore you to put my enquiry into deep thoughts, before replying, to see if your answer would resonate with mine.

The question is, ***what specific actions would you take if credible information reached you that in the next 40 days; will you go to your grave?***

Think deeply about this

Think again…

My assumption is you will spend those next 40 days with the people that matter, doing the things you love most. This is the same answer I often get from other people I ask.

The reason is people are people-centred, that is in relationships with other people you find fulfilment. Therefore, if this is how it works, then you have to learn to make relationships work.

Without this, how do we interpret living? We often find meaning in our contributions to everything around us not to ourselves. And for this reason, relationships need to be treated with utmost respect.

Put work and life in their respective positions

Whenever you give worktime to work and dedicate leisure time to the things that interest you, you get better results. Your happiness level increases, you make more money, and your health is insured.

You experience the contrary when you get both of them mixed up. When you say you want to work, take off every form of distraction and work, but, once you are done, rest. Prioritise your time and divide it, based on how important each part is, if for family do not lose it for anything else, if for work do not give it to anyone else, if you have not built a household yet, dedicate that time to explore other things that profits you.

This is how you build a life hinged on progress and great results. People who get results lower that what is expected often spend work time for leisure and they take leisure time working.

Your time at your place of business is not meant for after work discussions, which is the reason why there is time after work for discussions. If you keep giving time here and there for random conversations, you will get results lower than what you aimed for, at the beginning of the day. When you feel unsatisfied with what you got, you want to take it home to finish up, and with this, you are already eating into a time meant for something else.

Chapter seven

The habit of Character and Leadership

Our history in terms of experience and learning gave birth to all that we display today. We did not just become what we are, since what we are is simply an accumulation of days, months, and years of several experiences and what those experiences have turned into a pattern for our behavioural tendencies today.

Character in a lame man's understanding are the personality traits a human possesses. Character is the essential ingredient of one's behaviour. As humans, we all have a trait of good or bad; it is left to each one to exhibit what is of more valuable to them.

What is Leadership?

Leadership is having the ability to influence an individual or a group of people towards achieving a common goal. Take for example a business environment: it deals with having to instruct or giving directive information on how to re-strategise in a competitive situation. Leadership is also a process of motivating and inspiring people either based on original ideas or borrowed ideas to give a productive result.

Inasmuch as Character is an important trait, leadership is also important as well. Do you think one's Character is essential in leading? **Yes, it is**. Why? It is because the foundation or the first step of being a leader is having character traits that qualify you as a leader.

You would not give a large sum of money to someone you do not trust, wouldn't you? In addition, you cannot trust a mentally derailed person to give you directions on the road, because you do not trust his information.

One with a good character boasts of effective leadership because trust is built and definitely, without trust, there are no followers. Another way of describing a good character is to know what defines a trustworthy person, as we know that a good character breeds trust.

What makes people trustworthy?

1. They are reliable enough, due to the fact that they have exhibited behaviours showing reliability from passed situations.

2. They deliver as promised

3. They are truthful and honest in their dealings.

4. They are open to choices from others' perspective and make good decision.

Having looked at the features of trustworthiness, one may not be perfect enough but should have above 70%. A good character does not appear by nature, it is nurtured as a mother will nurse her suckling baby.

Leadership is simply putting up a show of great strategies to get a job done and exhibiting those ideas with good character trait. One's character is shown when we are faced with a difficult situation that challenges the principles or values and, going through with them, helps you to shape personally and professionally.

Why leadership is important

1. Leadership consists of more than one person.

2. It involves the intelligence of a person and level of maturity, which is not maturity certified by age, but qualified by character

3. Leadership has different styles and there is no best style because different situations bring different tactics one should use in settling each of them.

4. A leader has the ability to influence individuals or a group to achieve the desired goal.

5. Leadership is also a process of molding a person's behaviour, building the self-confidence of the employees, building the morale of the workers, thereby getting full cooperation to ensure effectiveness and efficiency.

6. Leadership provides guidance for the employees. A leader's role is not only to supervise but to guide the workers.

7. Good leadership motivates the subordinates, as they receive rewards from salaries and bonuses.

What qualifies a person to have some level of influence over other people is never in their portfolio. Although that serves as an addition people will follow for someone they love, and loving you means they accept, if not everything, but a large a chunk of your personality.

Characteristics of great leaders

1. A good leader is one who is not biased in dealings, decisions, or judgments; their decisions are based upon solid fact and reasoning.

2. A leader critically analyses the advantages and disadvantages of a situation, weighs them, and finds a favourable spot for everyone to land.

3. Great information relating skill is what promotes your leadership prowess. It is the ability to make good use of Communication skills, in relaying rules or policies to the team, workforce, board, and the public for a clear understanding of what is going on and what is expected.

4. Good leadership brings about accountability and a sense of obligation or duty towards the goals of the organisation. By this, the workers are motivated to obtain efficiency and effectiveness.

5. A good leader builds his self-morale to gain the faith of those he shields. Once you allow situations and challenges to

reduce your level of confidence, it reflects on your followers because they can sense that you are struggling to find courage

6. Leaders instill the sense of having to comprehend the problems of their employees. This helps to build a strong healthy relationship among their workers.

7. A leader can plan for extensive paths.

Most millionaires have common traits. Excluding a related range of bank account balance, courage, passion, vision are some units of these peculiarities.

These millionaire traits are also traits you find in the lives of those who have grown to become both powerful and influential leaders.

What are the millionaire traits?

1. Thinking Independently: Millionaires do not think only about money, they also think of creating new paths for those coming behind. Thinking independently is about being courageous enough to follow the path you created to get to your financial liberty.

Elon Musk today has created the world's first renewable rockets, his automobile company, Tesla made the world's first electric-powered car. It all depends on daring to think about new possibilities.

2. Vision and Passion: Having the foresight about their big dream that will come true eventually. Goals are being set in order to attain the height. Having the passion to forge ahead not just because it is expected but because it creates room for creativity and innovative ideas, which aid development of the thinking capacity of the employees.

This style is making the employees do a workshop on how to carry it out but doing what they are asked to do.

Leadership styles

Over time, we have had several people grow up to amass some level of both positive and negative influence and power. These people came with different approach, in order to get their desired results that made impact on our world. Let me share seven of such styles with you

1. Affiliate style: This leadership style is one in which a leader creates an opening for personal relationships with his employees/followers. A leader with this kind of style pays due attention to his employees and supports them, is genuinely concerned about their needs. It demands that you have a strong team collaboration spirit with you employees; it fosters harmony and encouragement amongst the team. In addition, your employees feel free to express themselves, whenever they think an idea is great or not and whenever they need to talk about a displeasure.

2. Autocratic style: This is the *"in-charge"* pattern where a leader sees himself as the smartest. Decisions are taken without or with little effort of the employees. Although one can dive into autocratic style where there is an important decision to be made at the moment and you have the deepest insights on it or when working with new employees who are not familiar with their duties, it is not a style of leadership you want to adopt generally. Leaders who make more impact are known to keep others in the loop, not going around dictating how affairs will run.

3. Authoritative styles: They are visionaries, confident in leading, people who pave the paths and put in place high expectations. Also, they are responsible for engaging and motivating their followers. They aid them in creating a foresight of the paths to be towed by the establishment to make its desired state a presence.

5. Pacesetting styles: This is like a racing style. They push their employees to work as fast as possible. While this style can be of advantage to the vision of the company in terms of speed, it is very hurtful to the employees.

Employees tend to get easily stressed under this type of leadership, which must be avoided. You are that leader who is empathetic and diplomatic in his approach.

6. Laissez-faire style: This involves working with highly experienced workers. It requires constant feedback. In this style of Leadership, employees are free birds without directions, which causes a shift in relation to the goal of the business. To prevent a drift, effective monitoring of the team members is active.

7. Coaching style: In this type of leadership, leaders tend to see the potentials of the employees. They assume that all the employees need is a guide and direction on how to explore in their ability which enables them to achieve their desired goals.

To know the leadership styles to use in different situations is also a characteristic of being a good leader. To be able to lead effectively with any of the styles, enhances good leadership.

To know this, one has to;

1. Understand their personality by asking colleagues around what strength they see, taking assessments on leadership styles.

2. Have complete knowledge of all the leadership styles: Be familiar with the different leadership styles and which can work at a given situation.

3. Be Genuine: any leadership style taken on by the leader must be open and transparent.

Reasons a leader could fail

Once you have earned a position of leadership, it does not mean you will be immune to downside, especially when you lack character traits, such as communication, humility, and ability to accept change. There are so many reasons why anyone can experience darkness in their leadership journey but I will share five.

1. **Selfishness:** they begin to become hungry for power. They tend to forget the responsibilities on their shoulders and start to fend for themselves only.

2. **Lack of vision and foresight:** when the leader is okay with the level of the company or group, they stop leading the people on how to aim higher or track record of the company's progress.

3. **Lack of communication:** the employee loopholes to do whatever they want. Communication can be

done through any means, such as emails, conference meetings.

4. **Inability to adapt:** the world advances every day, if you move with advances it may be difficult to put the employees in line with where the company is advancing to.

5. **Lack of criticism:** an Affiliate leader will have or may have a hard time on speaking on the weakness of the team or individual weakness, because they want to please them in every way which is not effective.

To summarise, character is an important ingredient in leadership. A passage of the Bible says "study to show thyself approved", which means that working hard enough to be qualified, your character will first qualify you before any other thing.

Character brings about credibility, loyalty, trust, integrity. Being intelligent or having a qualified skill becomes a waste without a good character, because those with such skills and good intelligence can get to the top, but what keeps them there will be characters exhibited. To gain followers is to nurture your character.

Help others grow, respect their feelings, build their self-esteem and watch them open doors for you.

Reread the book everytime you need!

"The future belongs to those who believe in the beauty of their dreams"

(Eleanor Roosevelt)

"Its always seems impossible until it's done."

(Nelson Mandela)

"You can't cross the sea marely by standing and staring at the water"

(Rabindranath Tagore)

"There are two rules in life. Number one: never quit; Number two: never forget rule number one."

(Duke Ellington)

www.ingramcontent.com/pod-product-compliance
Lightning Source LLC
Chambersburg PA
CBHW031436210526
45464CB00005B/2233